Jobs from A to Z

By Allison Mangrum
Illustrated by Gina Capaldi

To Derek, who works so hard to provide for our family.
—A.M.

With much love to my son, Cory.
—G.C.

Managing Editor: Patrice Gotsch
Editor: Kristin Belsher
Graphic Design: Danielle Arreola
Technical Printing and Pre-Press Coordinator: Kathy Styffe
Desktop Publishing Specialist: Ronaldo Benaraw
Editorial Staff: Heera Kang, Roberta Stathis, Linda Mammano, Rebecca Ratnam

Copyright © 2005 Ballard & Tighe, Publishers,
a division of Educational IDEAS, Inc.

2006 Printing

Catalog #2-370   ISBN 1-55501-675-8

Jobs from A to Z

A is for the **archaeologist** who finds clues to our past.

B is for the **bus driver** who makes sure we get to class.

2

C is for the **computer engineer** who makes a fast machine.

D is for the **dentist** who keeps my teeth straight and clean.

E stands for the **electrician** who makes sure our homes have light.

4

F is for the **firefighters** who put out fires day and night.

G is for the **geologist** who likes to study rocks.

H is for the **hairstylist** who cuts my curly locks.

E
F
G
H

I stands for the **inventor** who makes things we can use.

9

J is for the **journalist** who writes the daily news.

11 **K** is for the **kennel attendant**. He cares for our pets' needs.

L is for the **librarian**. He gives us books to read.

M is for the **mail carrier** who delivers a friendly letter.

12

N is for the **nurse** at school. She makes me feel much better.

O is for the **office assistant**. He writes and copies and types. 14

P is for the **plumber** who fixes leaky pipes.

Q is for the **quilter**, whose pretty blankets keep us warm.

R is for the **roofer**. His roofs protect us from the storm.

N O P Q R

S

stands for the **soldiers** who fight to protect our land.

T is for the **teacher** who helps us understand.

JOBS: A THROUGH Z

20

U is for the **umpire** who yells, "Strike three—you're out!"

V is for the **veterinarian** who helped heal my dog Scout. 22

W is for the **waiter** who serves us ice cream cones.

X is for the **x-ray technician** who takes pictures of our bones.

24

Y is for the **yard worker**. He plants flowers and prunes the trees.

Z is for the **zoo keeper** who feeds the bears and lions and monkeys.

S T U V

W X Y Z